Dedicated to
Lucas, Madison & Ansagan

Inspired by

The Falls of Feugh
Banchory, Aberdeenshire.

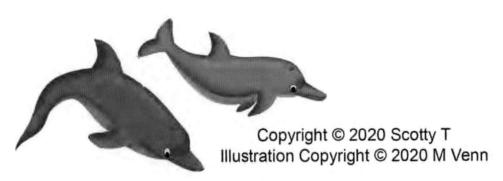

Little Smokie was a curious salmon
 that some fish thought unique...

But for every fish that thought this way,
 ten thought she was a freak!

The school of salmon laughed at Smokie and called her small and ugly,
They said her fins were far too big and showed their fins off smugly,

Their backs were sparkling silver fins, pink champagne across the belly...

Smokie's were grey above yellow and red, like concrete, custard and jelly.

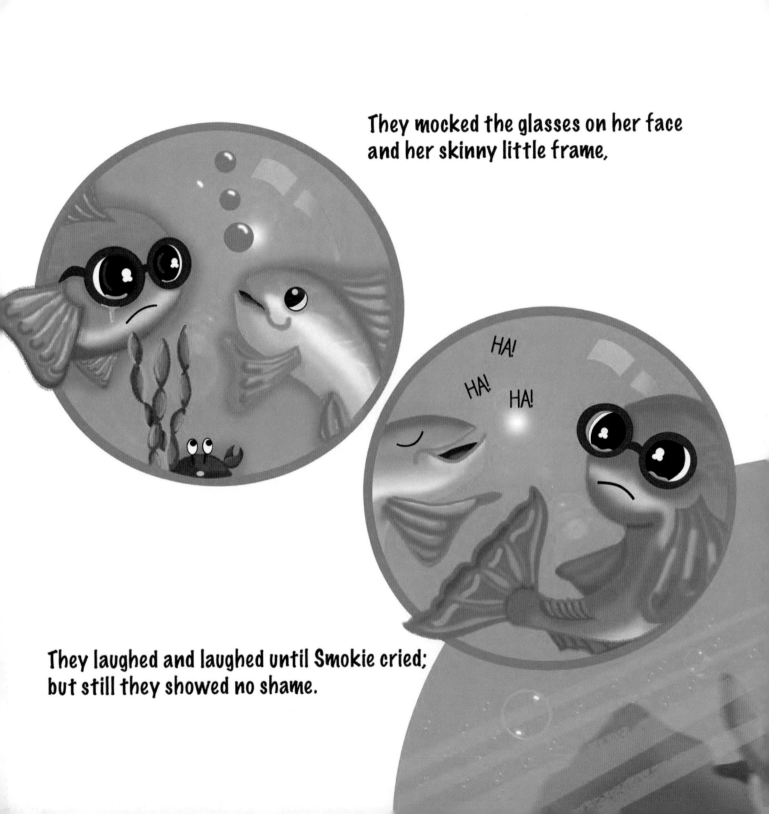

They mocked the glasses on her face
and her skinny little frame,

They laughed and laughed until Smokie cried;
but still they showed no shame.

She flapped her tail and off she sped,
avoiding a disaster,

Cutting through the sea like a torpedo,
no salmon could swim faster!

She swam and swam into Pearl the clam,
from who she would discover,
that her unique look was an entire book,
that shouldn't be judged by it's cover.

Pearl told of a journey that Smokie must make,
from the sea, upriver and back to the lake,
to lay eggs for her babies to spawn and grow,
where she was raised under a swan's shadow.

Good Luck!

Smokie took Pearl's advice and off she swam,
towards the school and away from the clam...

She continued to swim hard for many-a-mile,
zipping and zooming through slipstreams with guile.

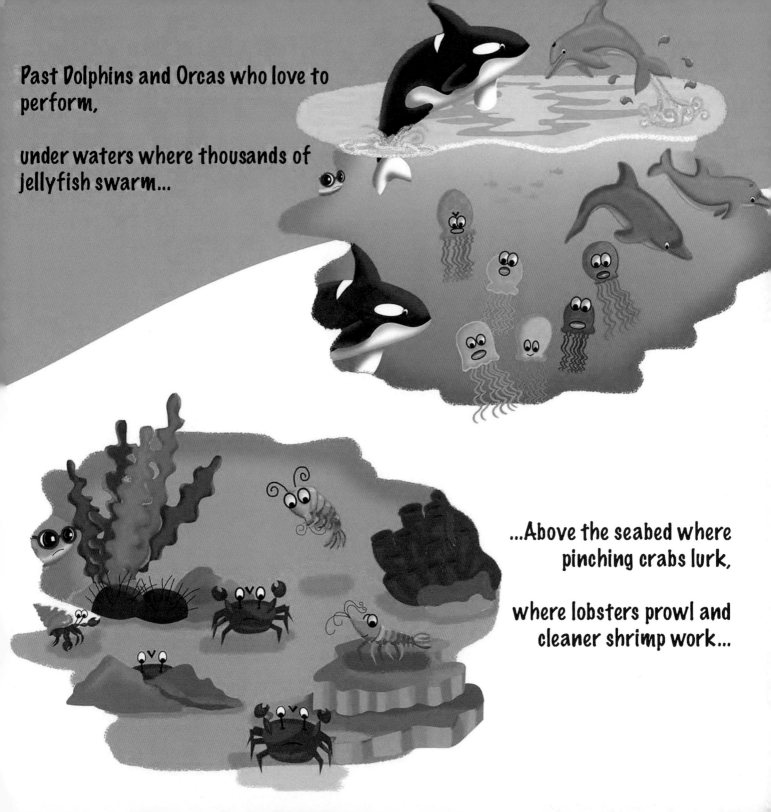

Past Dolphins and Orcas who love to perform,

under waters where thousands of jellyfish swarm...

...Above the seabed where pinching crabs lurk,

where lobsters prowl and cleaner shrimp work...

Just up ahead where waters collide,
a large pool of seals wait for fish
while they hide,
As the school draw nearer,
seals stay still and SHHHHHH!
patiently waiting to spring an

AMBUSH!

The seals make their move and zoom through the school,
gobbling up Salmon 'til their bellies are full.
But Smokie glides skillfully out of the cloud,
(her dull-toned scales were lost in the crowd)

Since silvery scales dazzle and glimmer,
seals seem to much prefer them for their dinner!

Upriver the current was fair, just the norm,
but this was the calm before the storm.
Up ahead water tumbles fast over falls,
crashing and splashing but that isn't all,

As well as the steep climb through multiple layers,
it's lined bank-to-bank with GRIZZLY BEARS!
Standing in rapids and keeping close watch,
for tired-looking Salmon that they can swatch!

Smokie swam down with the rest of the Salmon,
then leapt from the river as if shot from a cannon.

She leapt so high with her oversized fins,
straight over Mummy bear and her twins!

But waiting was Daddy Bear, his jaws open wide:
there seems no escape and nowhere to hide!
Then the sun caught the lens from the glasses she wears,
reflecting it's light into the eyes of the bear!

As Smokie returned to
the river with a splash,

the bear lost his footing
and fell in with a CRASH!

as Smokie watched on she hit a rock; WHACK!
remembering Pearl's words "DON'T LOOK BACK"

Long bends in the river led Smokie to a pond,

but isn't the water in which she was spawned,

There's no white-water rapids or waterfalls here,
a good place to rest for the final frontier!

A fly lands above with a delicate splash,
one hungry fish is there in a flash.

The fish opens wide and the fly disappears,
perfectly planned by the man with the beard,

On the boat up above with a rod and a net,
not to mention a bait-box with worms and insects...

Smokie continues to
follow the scent,

week-upon-week-upon-week
have been spent,

And mile-upon-mile-upon-mile
have been swam,

that started way back
on the words of a clam...

A journey that had its fair
share of scares,

from pods of seals to
sleuths of bears,

One final flip from the
stream to make,

and Smokie is home to
her swan-shadowed lake!

Printed in Great Britain
by Amazon